THE ROCKWELL MUSEUM

POETRY INSPIRED

BY THE

COLLECTION

POETRY INSPIRED

BY THE

COLLECTION

Presented by

THE ROCKWELL MUSEUM | CORNING, NY

Poetry by Michael Czarnecki

Forward by Kirsty Buchanan

ISBN: 978-0-9769919-8-4

Copyright © 2018. Produced by The Rockwell Museum, A Smithsonian Affiliate
111 Cedar Street | Corning, NY 14830
www.rockwellmuseum.org

Layout by Willa R. Vogel, The Rockwell Museum.

COVER IMAGE: Albert Bierstadt, *Mount Whitney*, circa 1877, oil on canvas, 68 7/8 × 116 5/8 in.
Rockwell Foundation Purchase. 78.14 F

FORWARD

Kirsty Buchanan
*Curator of Collections
and Exhibitions*

The Rockwell Museum is a community centered institution that freely engages our audiences to become participants in the visual arts. Our exhibitions and permanent galleries are curated to invite personal engagement and honest reflection. While we strive to provide an art historical interpretation of our collections, The Rockwell Museum also places great value on the individual response to art. No one response is "correct" or was conceived by the artist to be the "right" response. What you as a viewer bring to art has the potential to further enrich that object's cultural meaning for others. Art is intended to be activated through the dynamic partnership of audience.

Each poem in this book is a personal literary response to selected works within The Rockwell's permanent collection. They are the unique creation of one individual, Michael Czarnecki, one of our many local supporters. Harnessing the classical model of ekphrasis has provided an ancient precedent for this rhetorical exercise, whereby a written account is crafted in response to a visual work of art. Therefore, it is in the spirit of dynamic partnership that we present this first book of poetry inspired by The Rockwell Museum's collection for your enjoyment!

Clouds in the Canyon

Thomas Moran
1915
oil on canvas
20¼ × 25⅛ inches

Rockwell Foundation Purchase
78.43 F

clouds come sweeping in from the west
mist hangs low in the canyons
Bristlecone Pine towers above rocks

clouds come and go
mist ephemeral
Bristlecone hundreds of years old

all of this, a passing moment
to canyon rocks
millions of years here

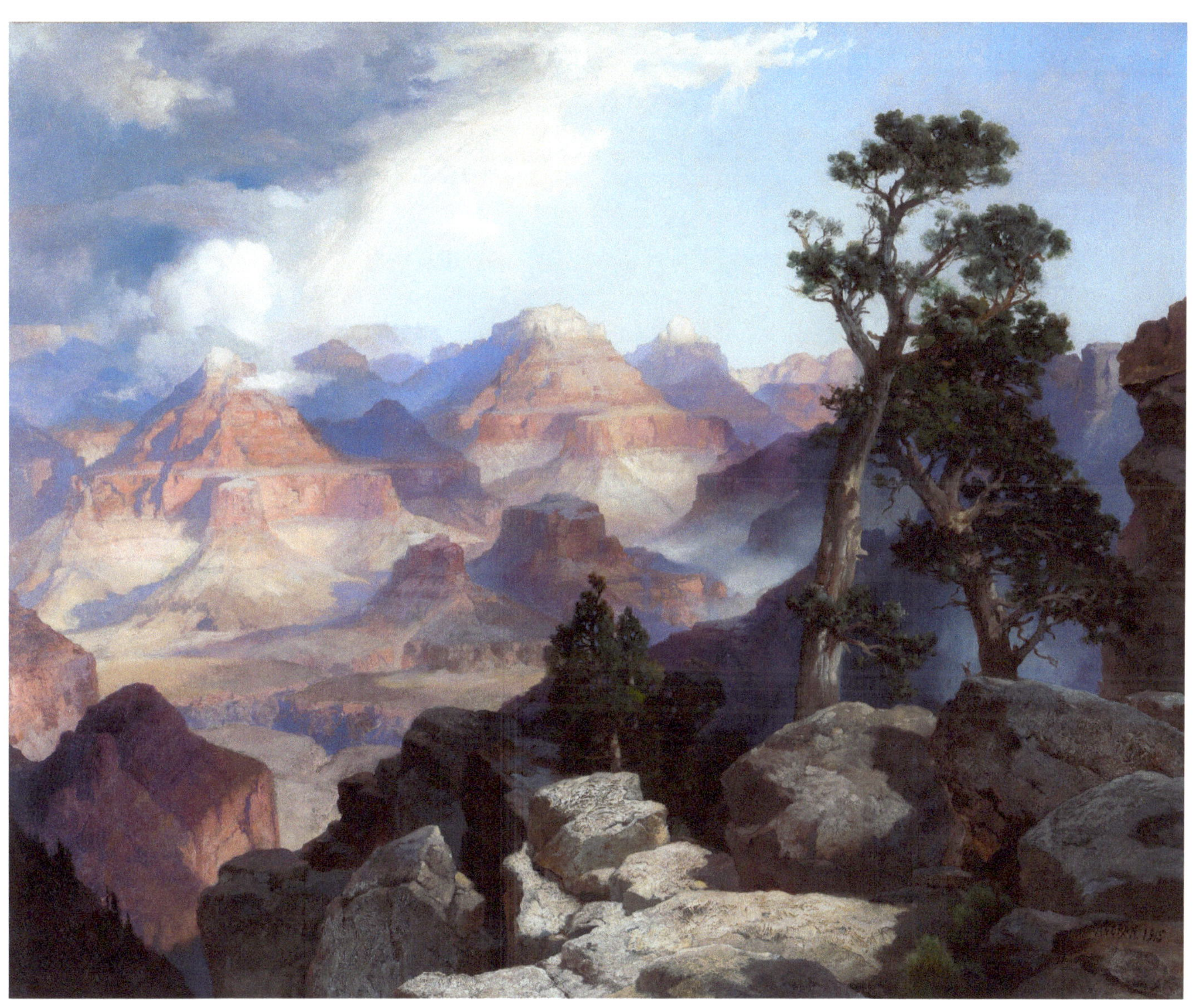

Jury for Trial of a Sheepherder for Murder

Ernest Leonard Blumenschein
1936
oil on canvas
46 × 30 inches

Clara S. Peck Fund Purchase
97.13 F

so these are the men that hold my fate
I choose not to cast my eyes down
I want to look at each and every one of them
one by one, down one row, back on the other
they each have faces that have seen much
faces that have witnessed life's ups and downs
I want the memory of those faces to go with me
wherever it is I will go after they decide
if back home, I will hold their faces close
if hanging from a gallows, I'll curse every one

I want to look directly into the eyes of just one
one who, like me, is a brother, a son, a father
one who can see beyond my face, see into my heart
if I can, maybe it is he who will save me from the noose

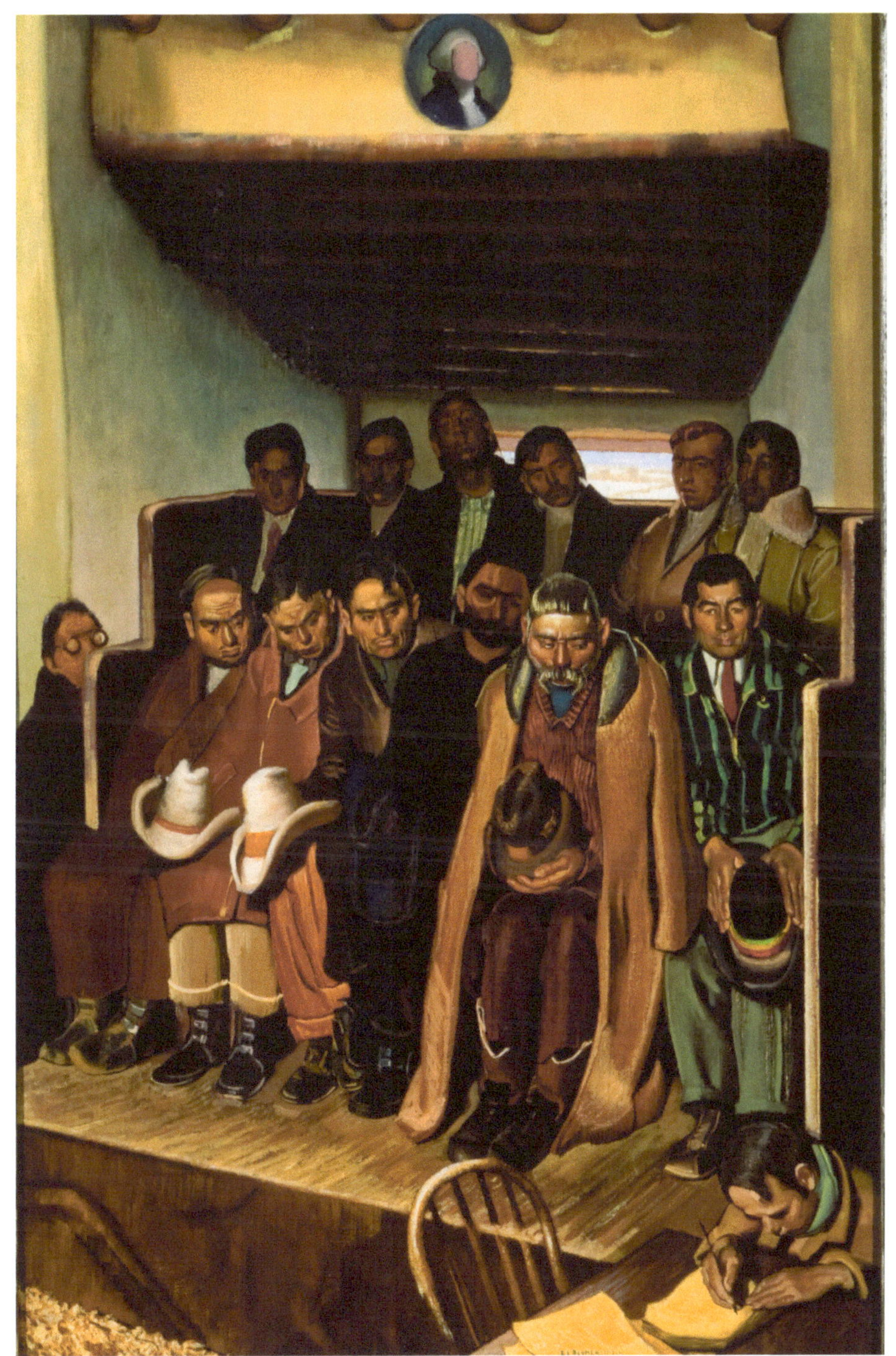

Mount Whitney

Albert Bierstadt
circa 1877
oil on canvas
68⅞ × 116⅝ inches

Rockwell Foundation Purchase
78.14 F

where do clouds end
mountains begin

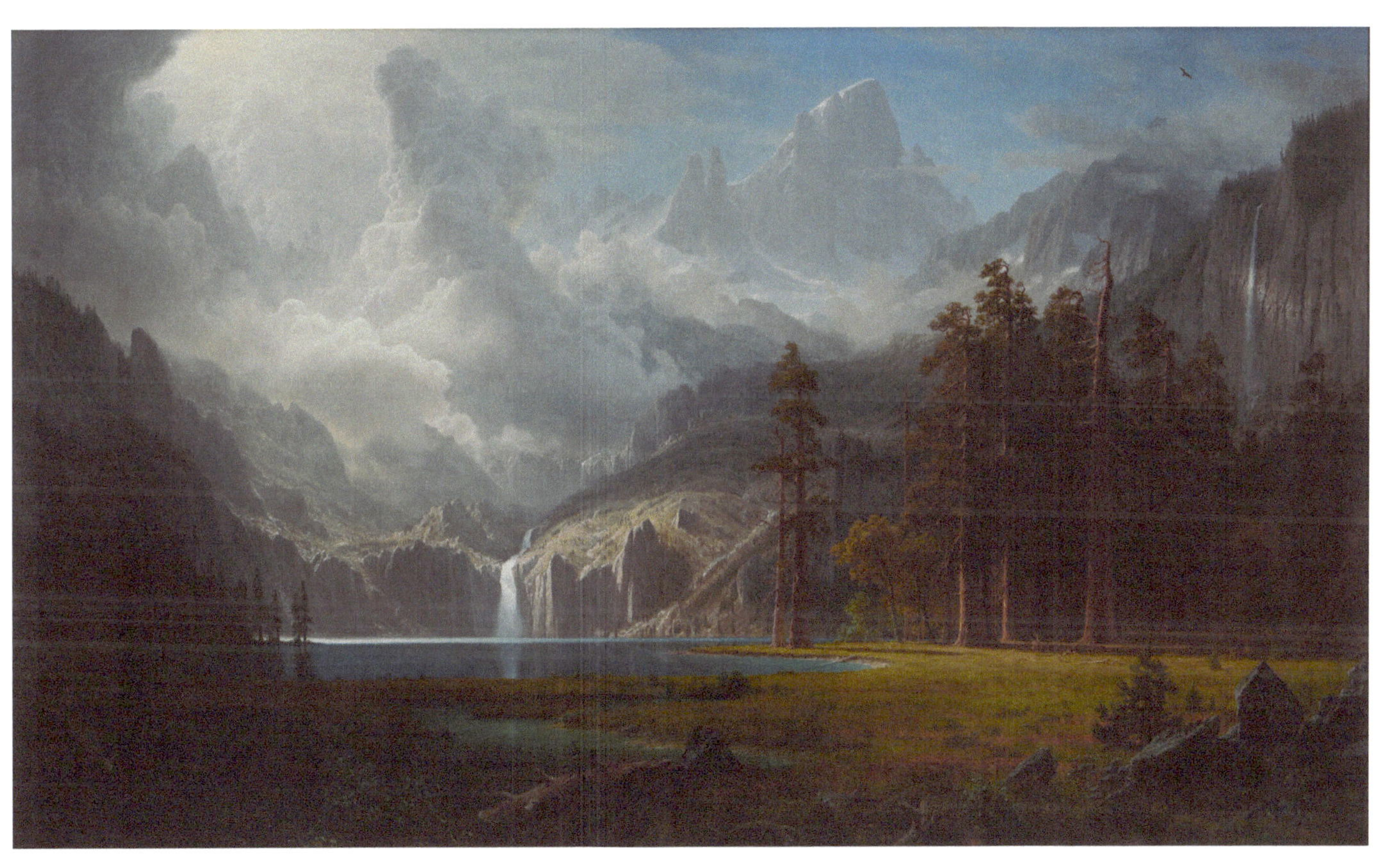

The Two Kings:
Corn and Cotton

Elizabeth H. Remington
1876
oil on canvas
36 × 26 inches

Clara S. Peck Fund Purchase
2015.2

surface seeing
two agricultural crops
one southern
one northern
one food
one clothing
a created scene
not seen in real life
a pastoral scene
pleasant in its simplicity

ah, but underneath
surface layer
so much being displayed
so much being said
so much being alluded to

almost a hundred fifty years ago
this painting spoke to differences
after Civil War, a country divided
this painting trying to heal wounds
viewing this painting now
who could see beyond surface

we've moved beyond
agricultural dominance
what divide needs mending now
what painting healing wounds
would be created today

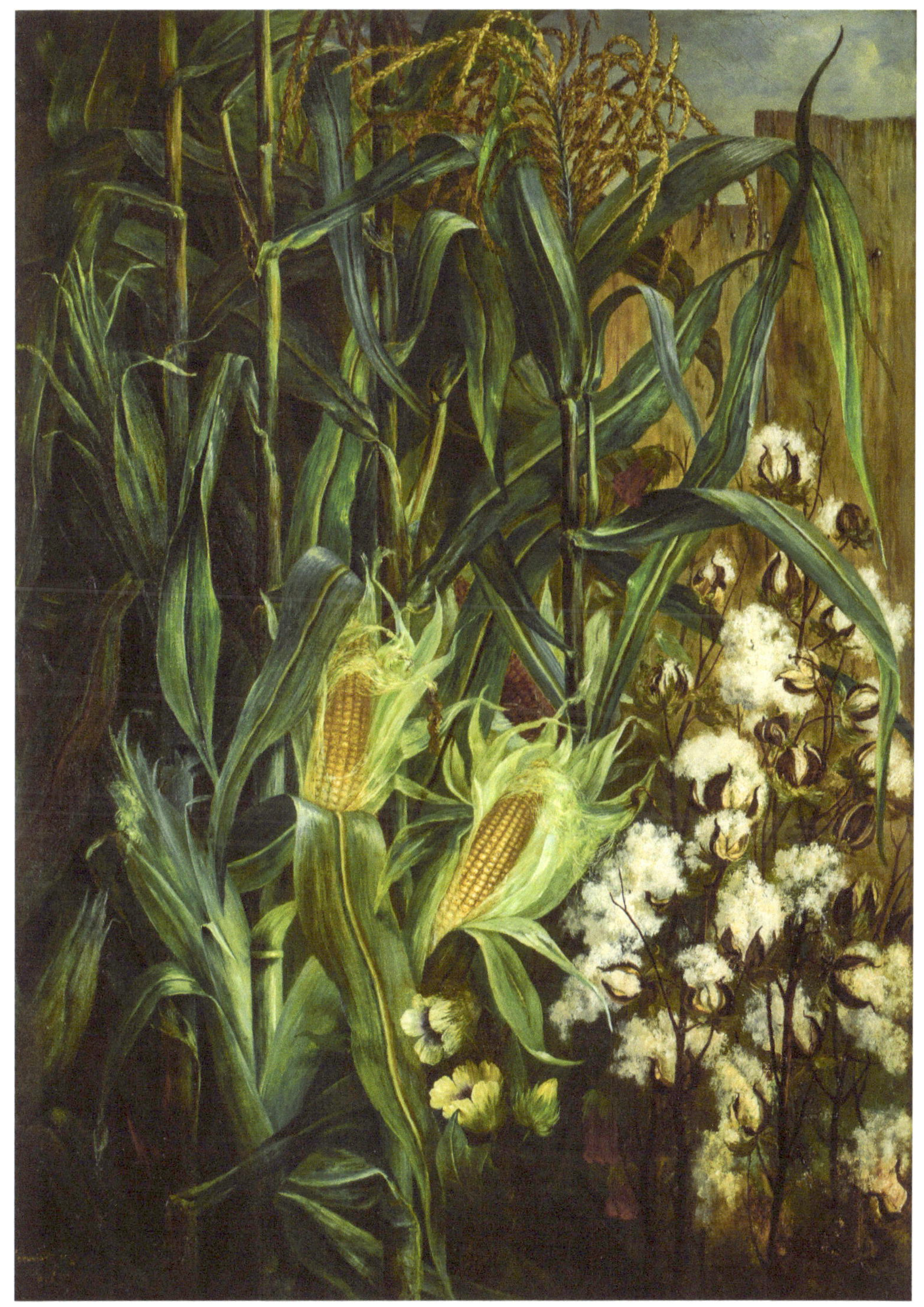

Indian Encampment on the Platte River, Colorado

Thomas Worthington Whittredge
circa 1875
oil on canvas
14½ × 22⅛ inches

Acquired with proceeds of 1992 and
1993 *Chili & Chocolate Roundup* and
additional funds
93.9 F

such a peaceful scene
distant mountains to the north
tipis in shade of cottonwoods
Platte River flowing slowly by
dogs playfully swimming
height of summer ease

yet, beyond distant mountains
upriver from where water flows
storm clouds are forming
not high in summer sky
but swelling on nearby ground
quickly expanding ever westward
a white tide of easterners
hungry for land, greedy for gold

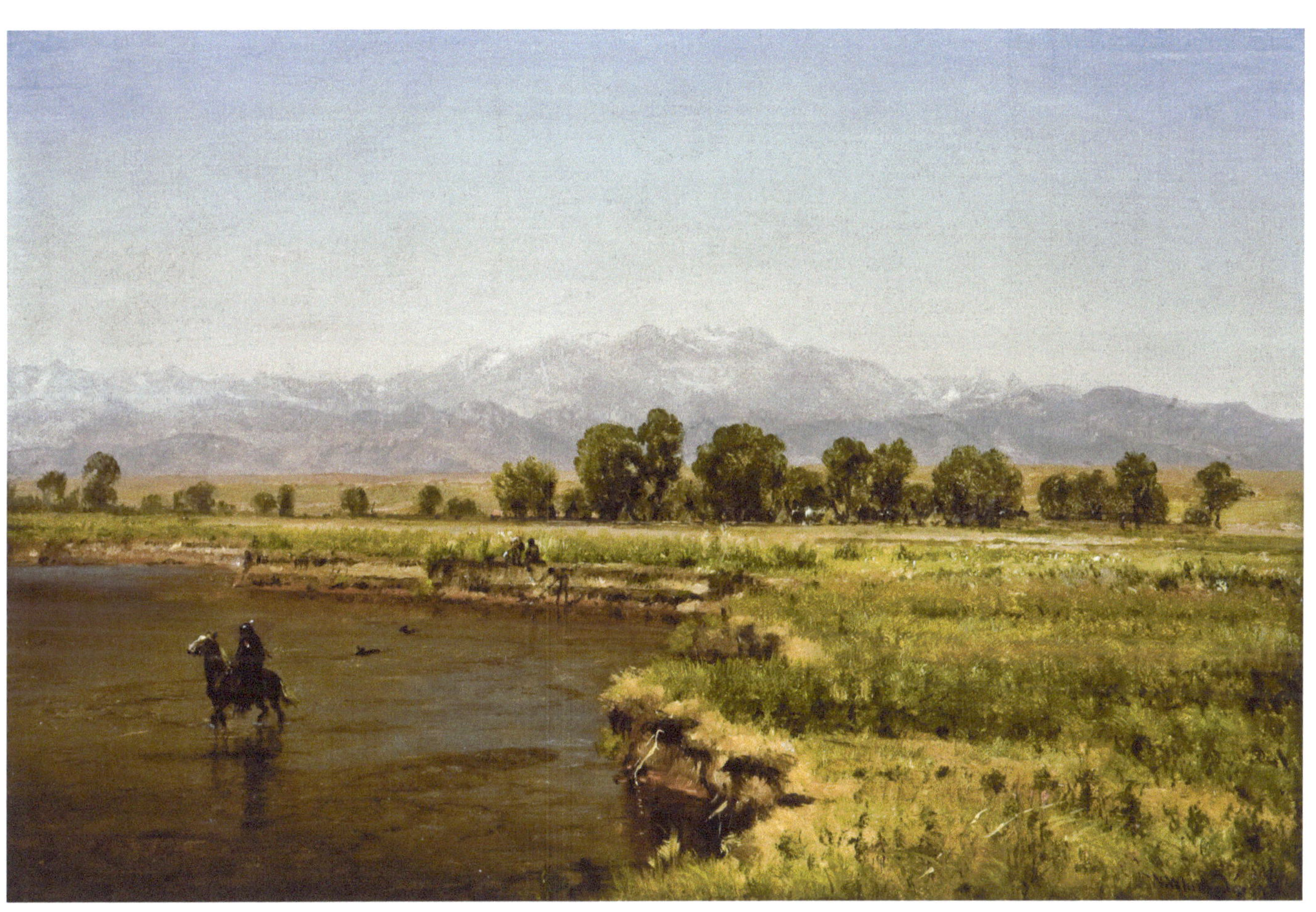

Yosemite

Thomas Hill
circa 1908
oil on canvas
56½ × 36⅛ inches

Gift of Hertha G. and Robert F. Rockwell, Jr.
91.94 F

immense presences
sheer cliffs
towering mountains
even Yosemite Falls
cascading over
two thousand feet
is dwarfed in comparison

how can one stand
among such presences
and not be humbled

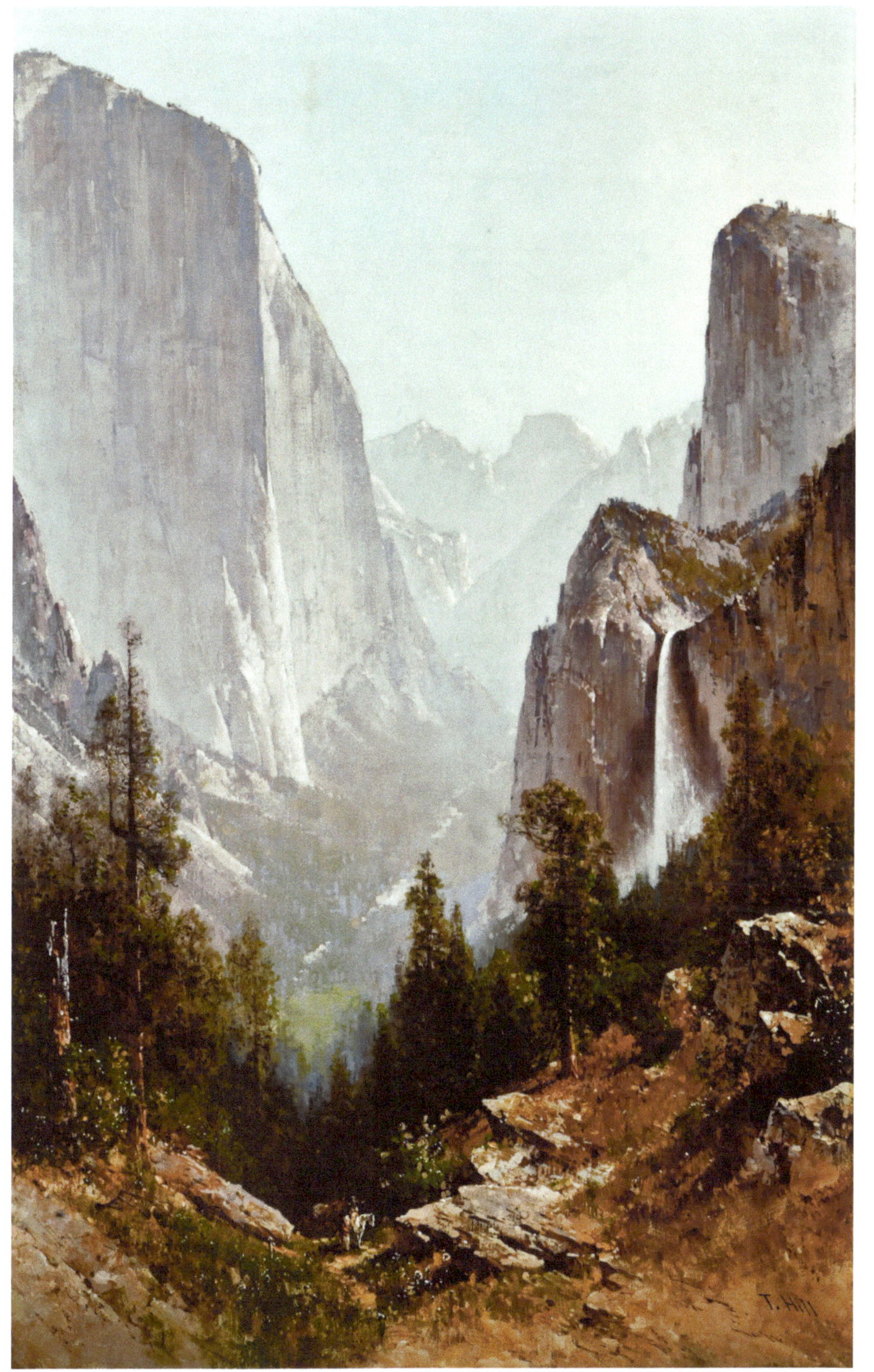

The Tanner

Seth Eastman
1848
oil on canvas
30½ × 25⅝ inches

Gift of Robert F. Rockwell, Jr.
78.29 F

already cool winds blow from the north
there is so much work to be done
more corn to be harvested
more hides to be tanned
soon cool winds will turn cold
snow will fly through the air
more food needs to be put up
more boots, clothing to be made
when the men return from their hunt
there'll be more hides to tan
more meat to cut up, dry
endless, this work before winter
yet, when snow piles high
clothing made, food preserved
there will be time to rest
time to tell stories of the old ways
time to be thankful
for what has been provided

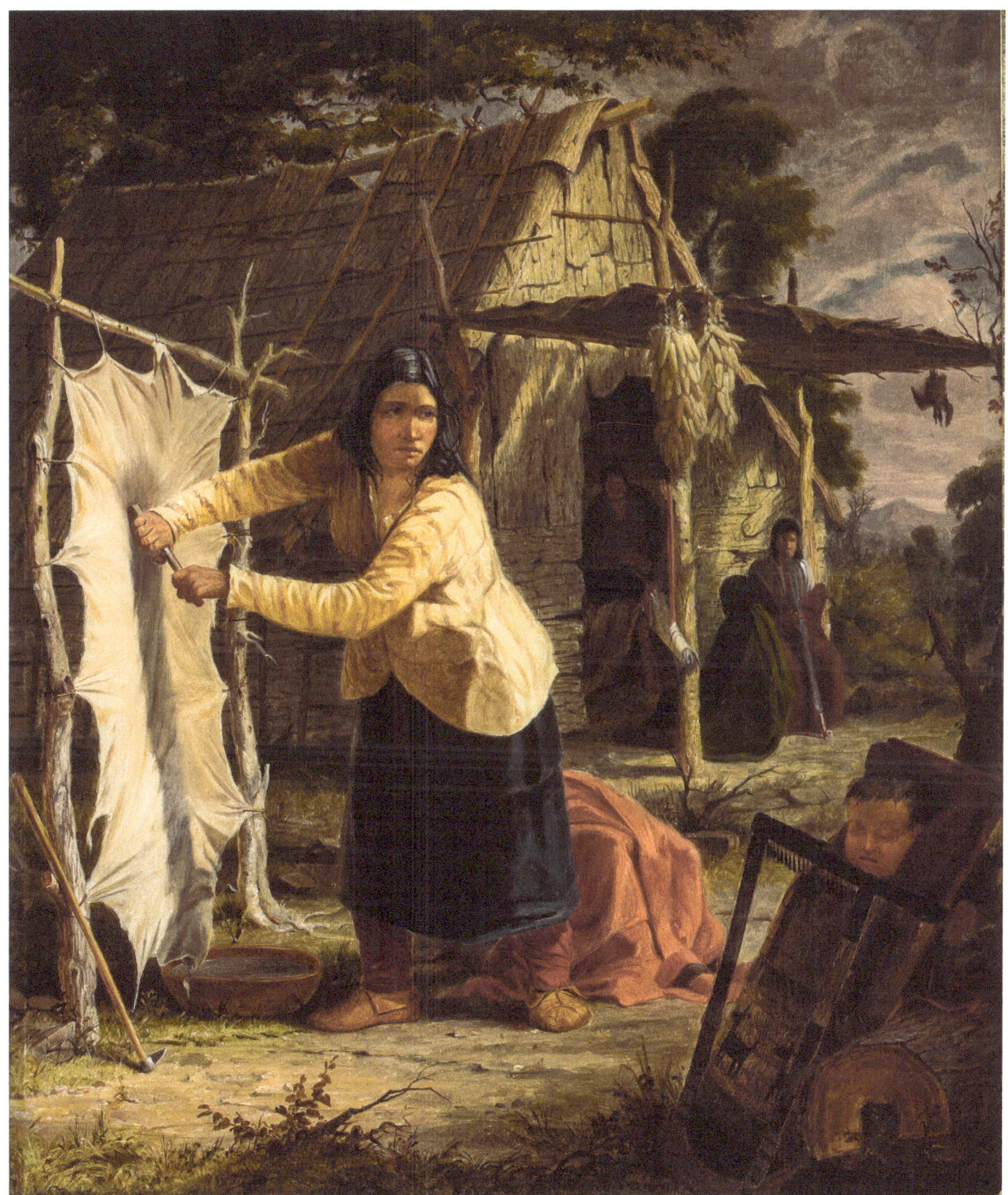

Little Mother

Abastenia St. Leger Eberle
modeled 1907, cast 1911
bronze
12⅞ × 3¾ × 3⅝ inches

Museum Purchase through Funds
from the Silver Dollar Society
2017.13

it doesn't matter where in the world
it doesn't matter when in the world
some things are eternal

it doesn't matter how rich you are
it doesn't matter how poor you are
some things are eternal

it doesn't matter if you live in the country
it doesn't matter if you live in the city
some things are eternal

it doesn't matter what color you are
it doesn't matter what ethnicity you are
some things are eternal

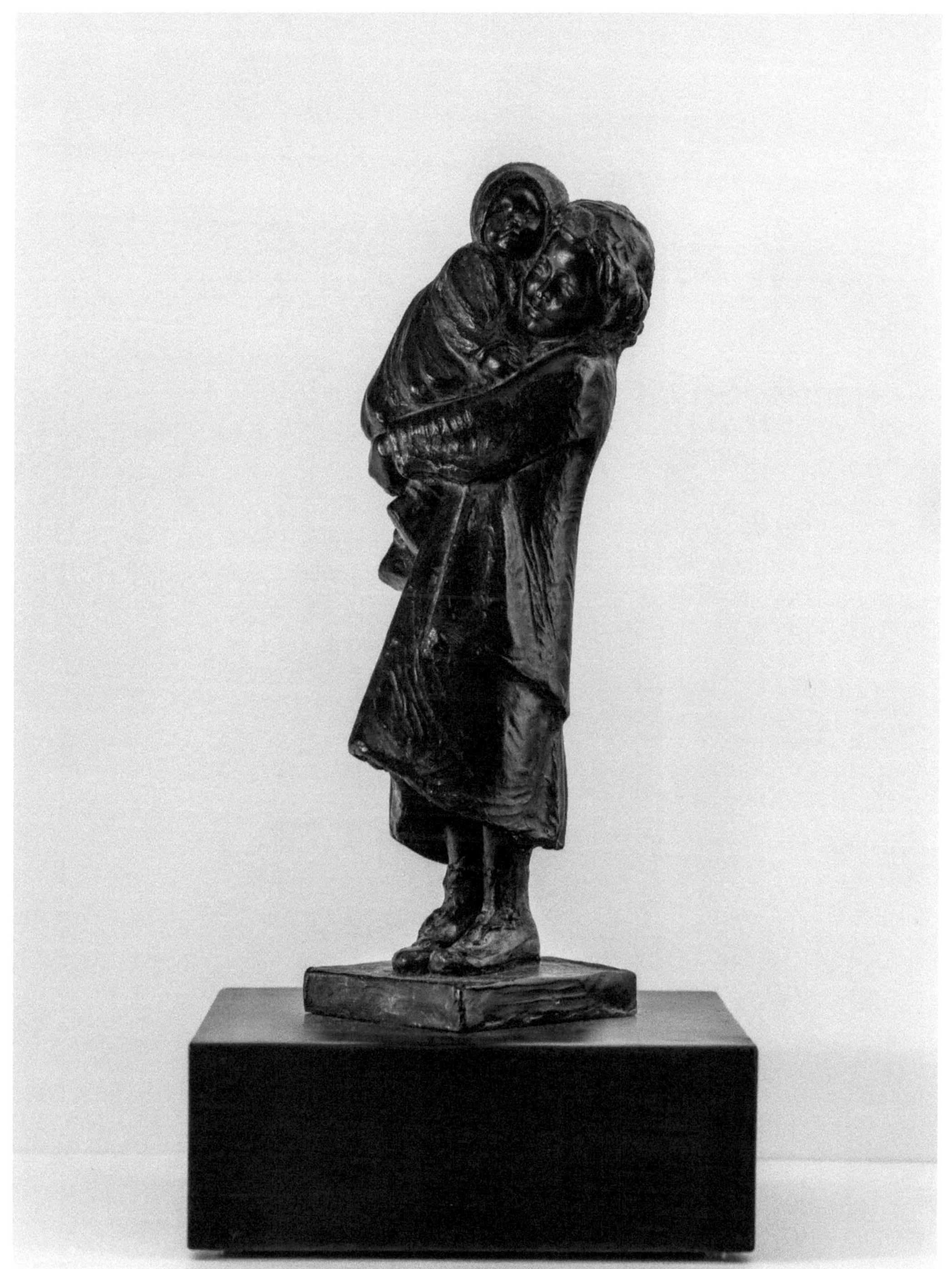

Hanover Square

Louis Lozowik
1929
lithograph on paper
18⅜ × 13⅛ inches

Clara S. Peck Fund Purchase
2017.9.6

© Courtesy of the estate of Louis Lozowick
and Mary Ryan Gallery, New York.

mid-morning
New York City
hustle, bustle
toot, toot, toot
constant stream of cars, trucks
rumble, rumble, rumble
as train passes by
people coming, going
continually
eternal movement
eternal sound
eternal freneticism
in this city that never sleeps

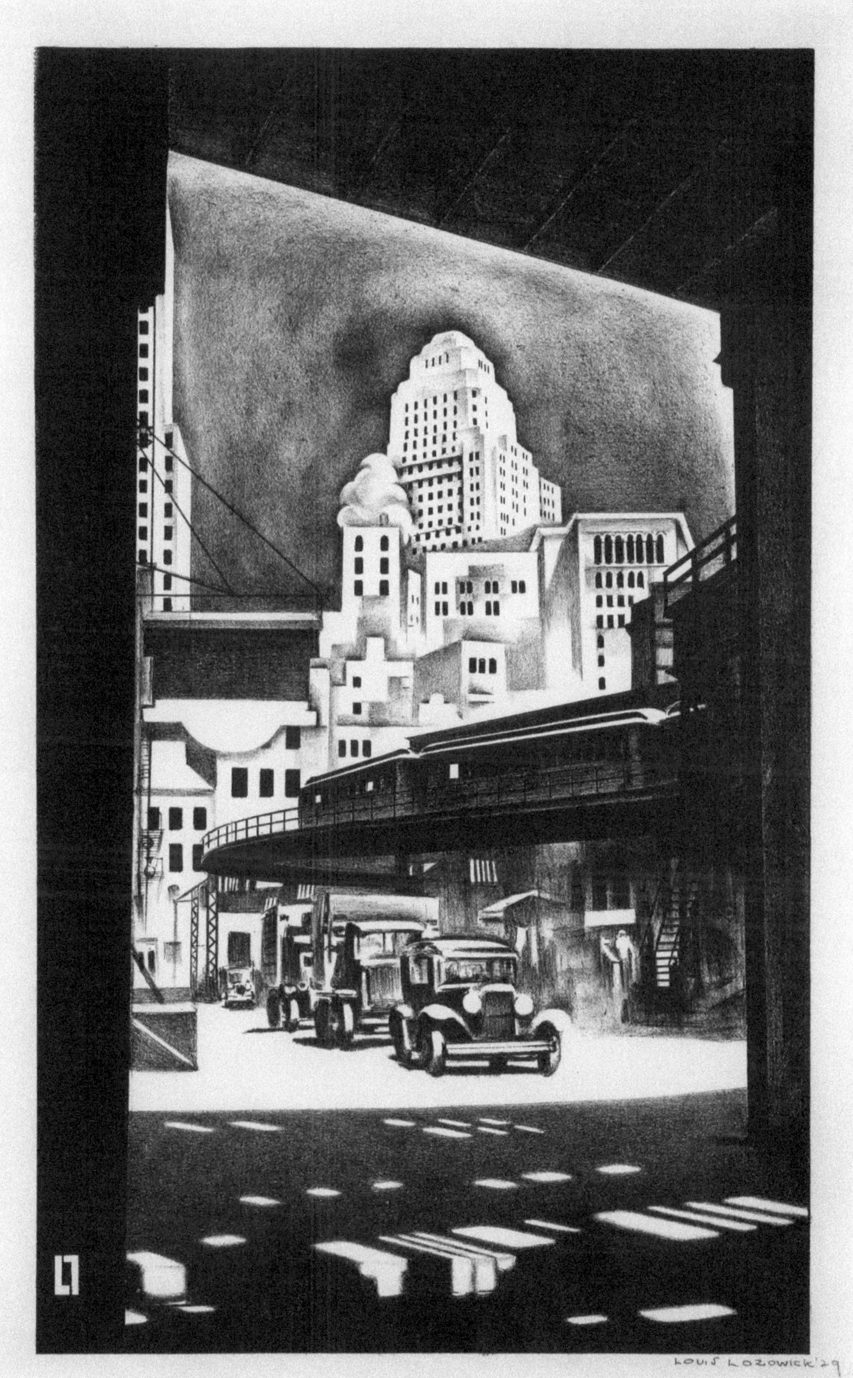

LOUIS LOZOWICK '29

Hey (The Langston Hughes Series)

Benny Andrews
2005
oil on paper, painted fabric, paper collage
22½ × 15 inches

Clara S. Peck Fund Purchase
2017.14

sun's a setting
keep singing them blues

sun's a rising
them blues gone away

moon's a rising
owl's hooting away

moon's a setting
start of a new day

rain's a falling
let's hurry inside

rain's a stopping
let's go back outside

piano man's playing
let's get up and dance

piano man's singing
it's time for romance

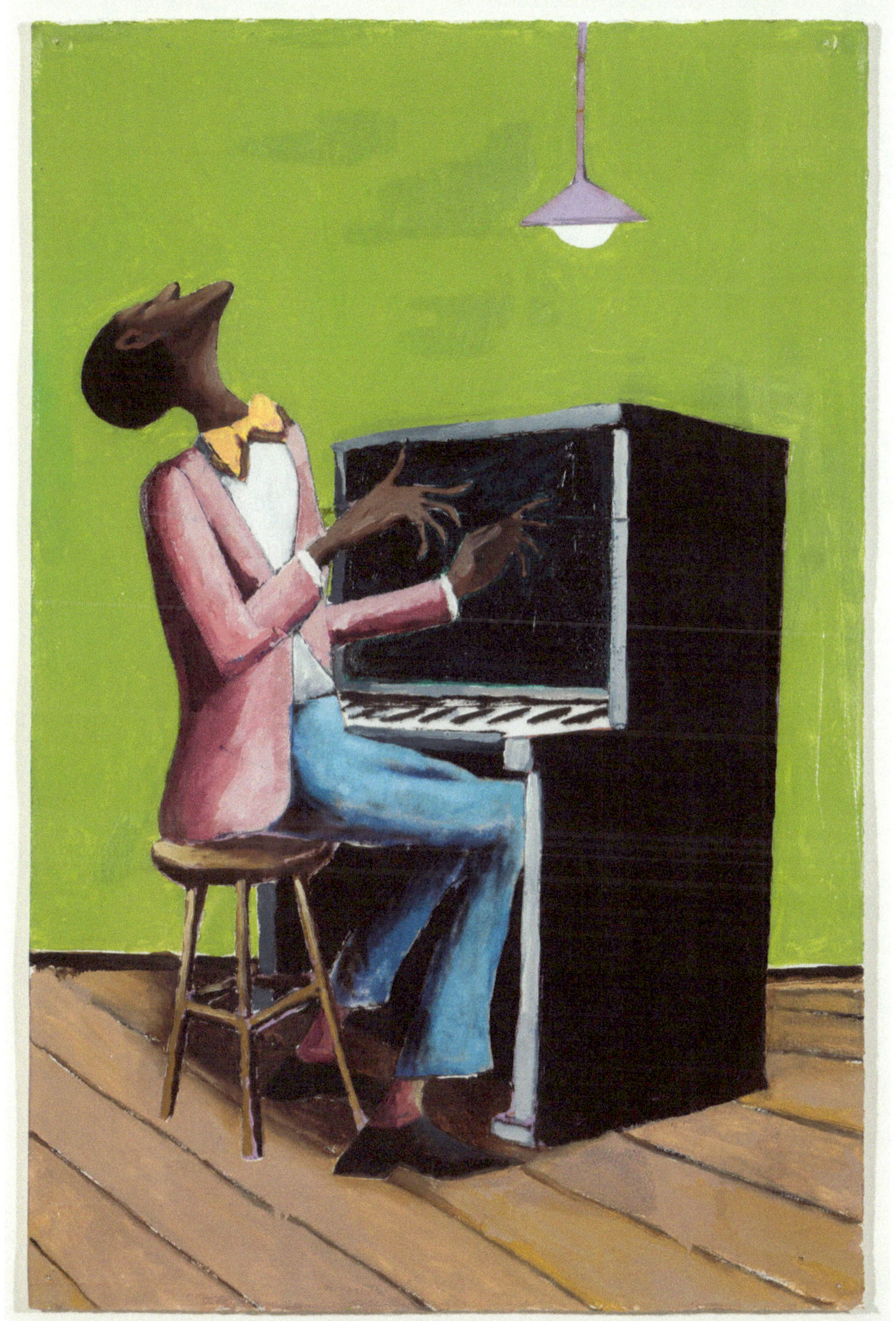

George Figured a Course From the Heavens, and Found It Took Him Nowhere

Harvey Thomas Dunn
1910
oil on canvas
24 × 36 inches

Museum Purchase
83.39 F

ok, so we've been walking for hours
I thought I knew the way back to camp
Big Dipper pointing to the North star
but it's all so different being on foot
why are we all such bad poker players
losing three horses in one night
then we stayed too long at the saloon
drowning out our losses with whiskey
hey guys, trust me for a little bit more
if we don't find camp in an hour or so
we'll find some soft ground to lie down on
try to catch a little sleep if we can
things will look a lot different in morning light

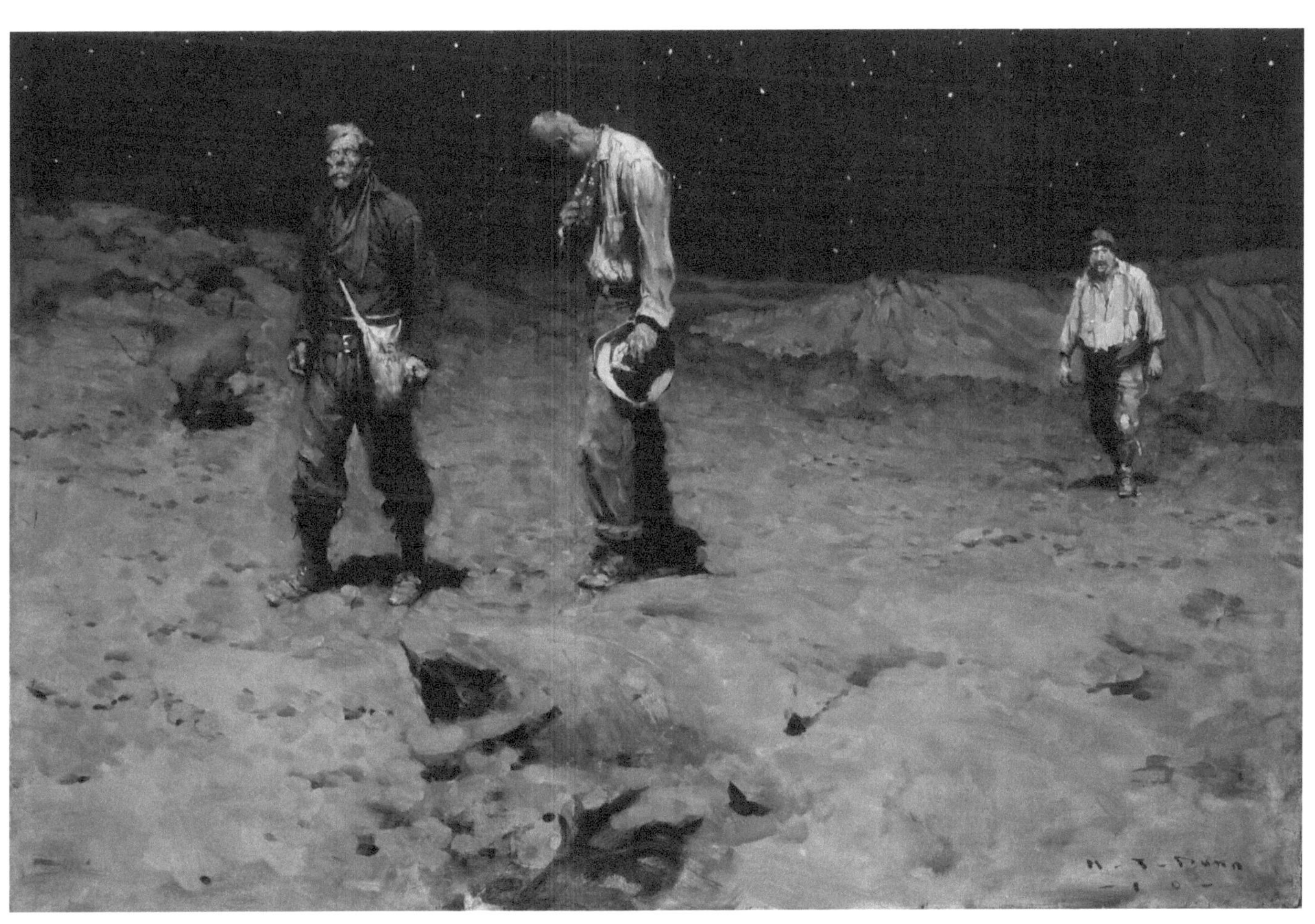

Winter in Zion

1987
Clyde Aspevig
oil on canvas
48⅛ × 54⅛ inches

Museum Purchase
88.6 F

these mountains, this park
so crowded at other times
here now, in winter
so few visitors
space to be alone
take in this seasonal splendor
time to just be with mountains
to contemplate, meditate
watch shadows move slowly
over snow pack, granite cliffs
to stand still, breathe in
brisk, cold mountain air
to feel silence of landscape
that is so hard to discover
at other times of year

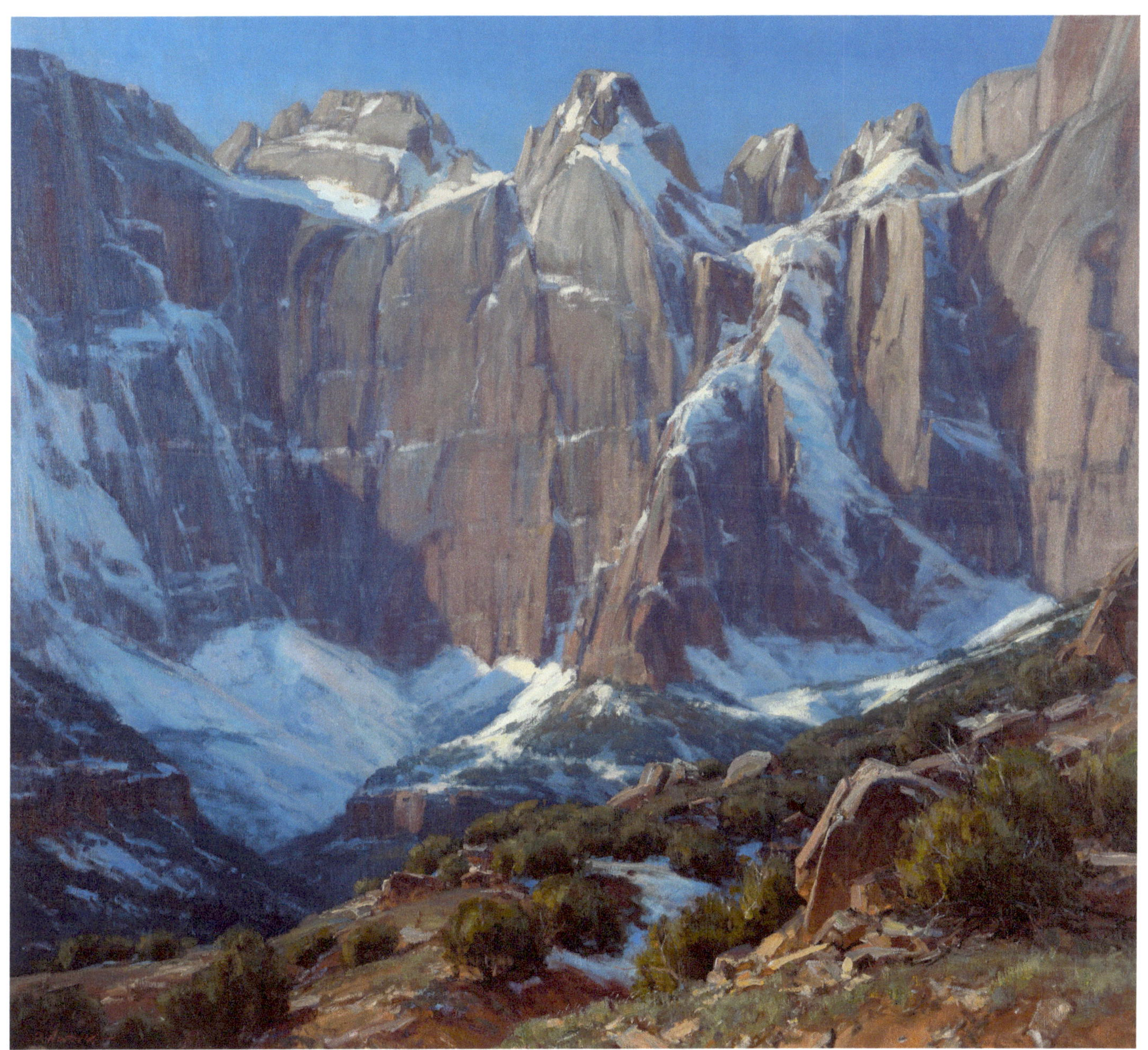

Nevada Fall, Yosemite

not just the view
even more so, the sound
a rushing roar
heard long before
water even seen
water falling, rumbling
tumbling over rocks
down precipices
drowning out
bird song
squirrel chatter
constant vociferousness
in a language
we can only hope
to understand

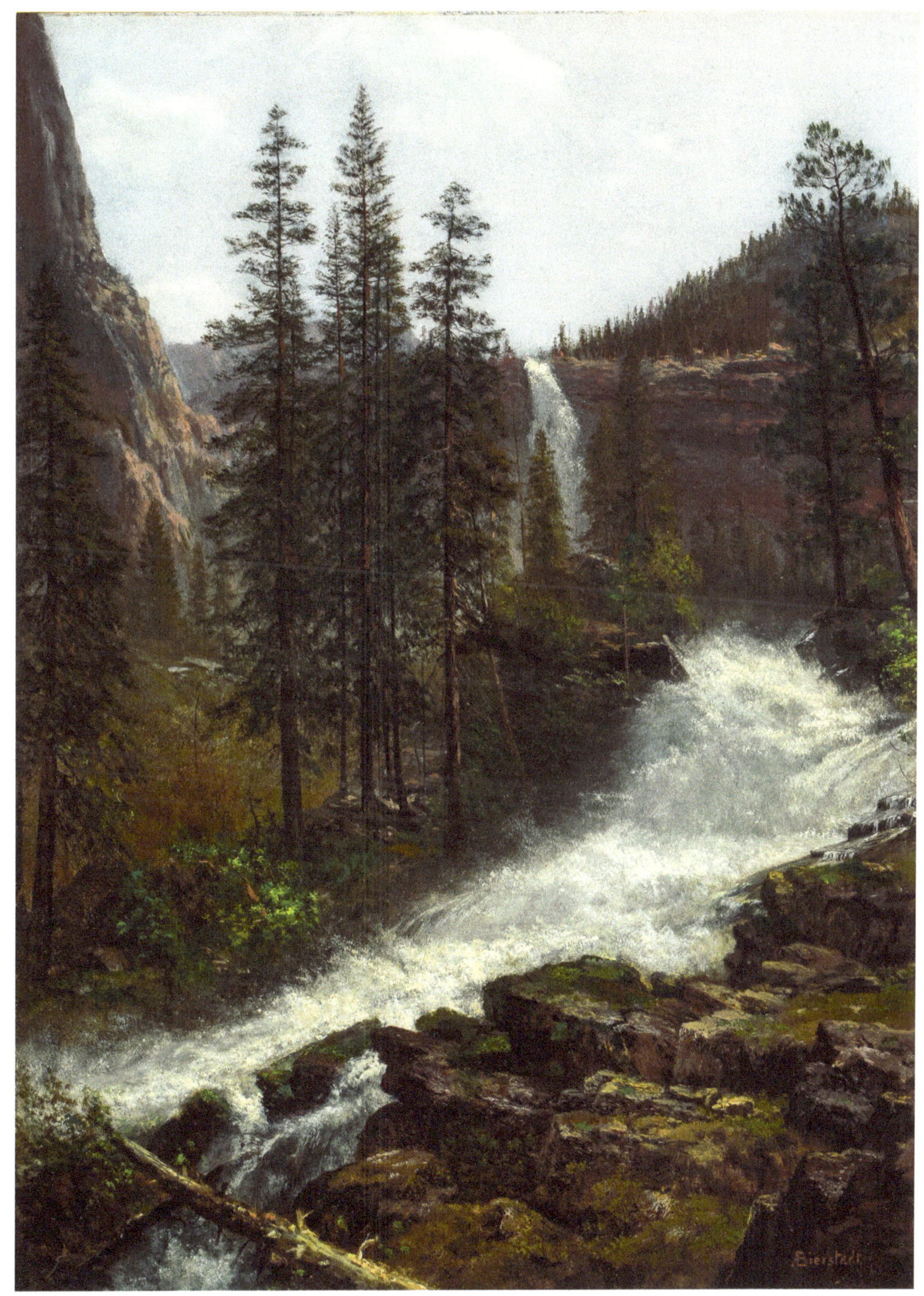Bierstadt

Ojibway Indian Spearing the Maskenozha (Pike)

Frank Earle Schoonover
1923
oil on canvas
40⅜ × 30¼ inches

Clara S. Peck Fund Purchase with
assistance of Mr. and Mrs. Clint Janes for
conservation and framing
97.1 F

stillness of water
stillness of Ojibway
suspended animation
eyes intently focused
body intensely focused
three-pronged spear
ready to be thrust downward
at precisely the right moment
this maskenozha a gift
fish-being giving its life
to sustain life of human being

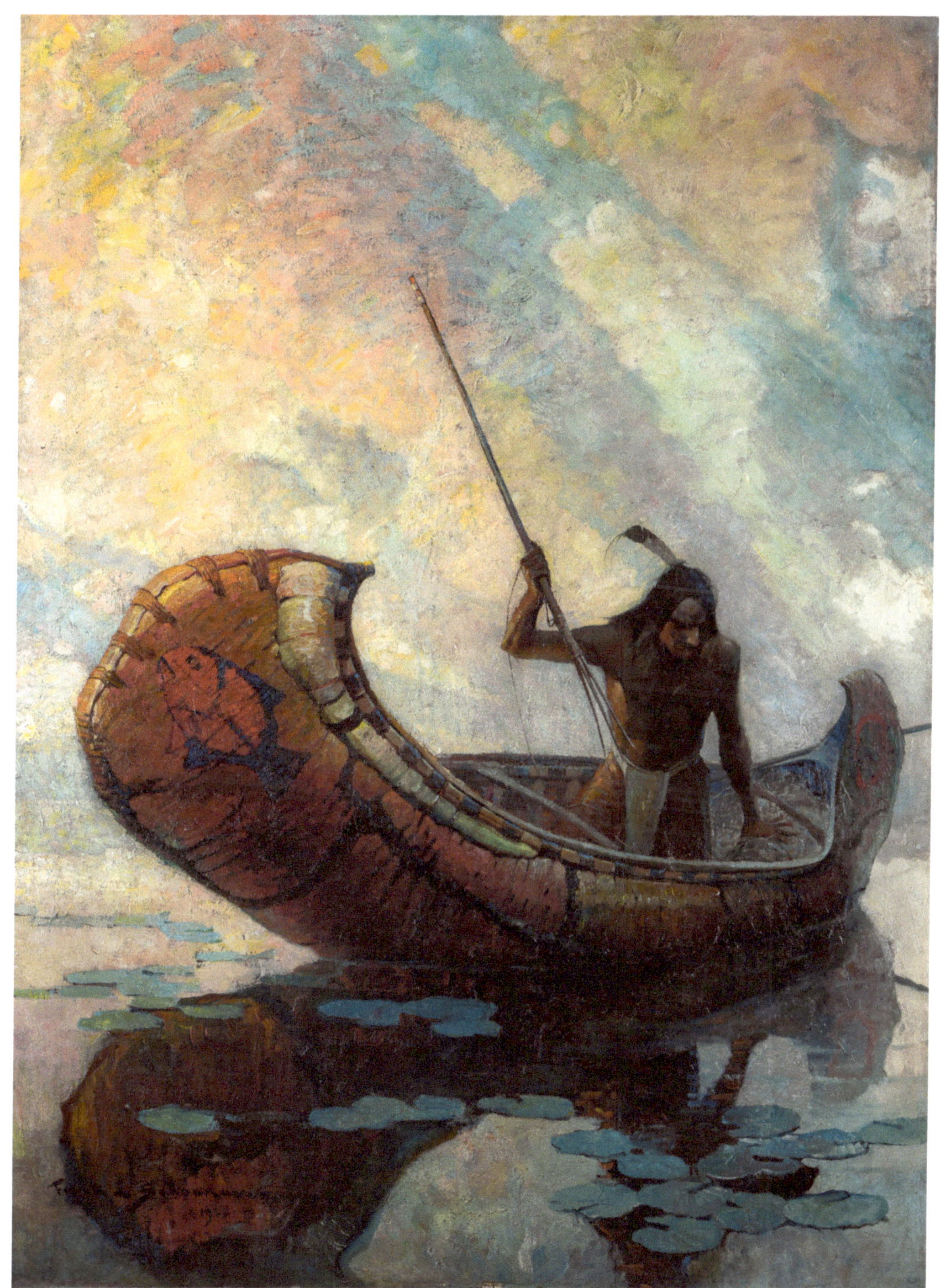

Indian Canoes on the Columbia River

Cleveland Salter Rockwell
1883
oil on canvas
28¼ × 48⅛ inches

Gift of Sandra Rockwell Herron
91.63 F

already settlers have arrived
their fires burn across wide river
their large boats come and go
how many more springs, summers, autumns
gathering berries, harvesting wild plants
fishing for salmon, will we have before
white men crowd us out, spoil the rivers
destroy the forests, tear down the mountains

I only wish this was a dream

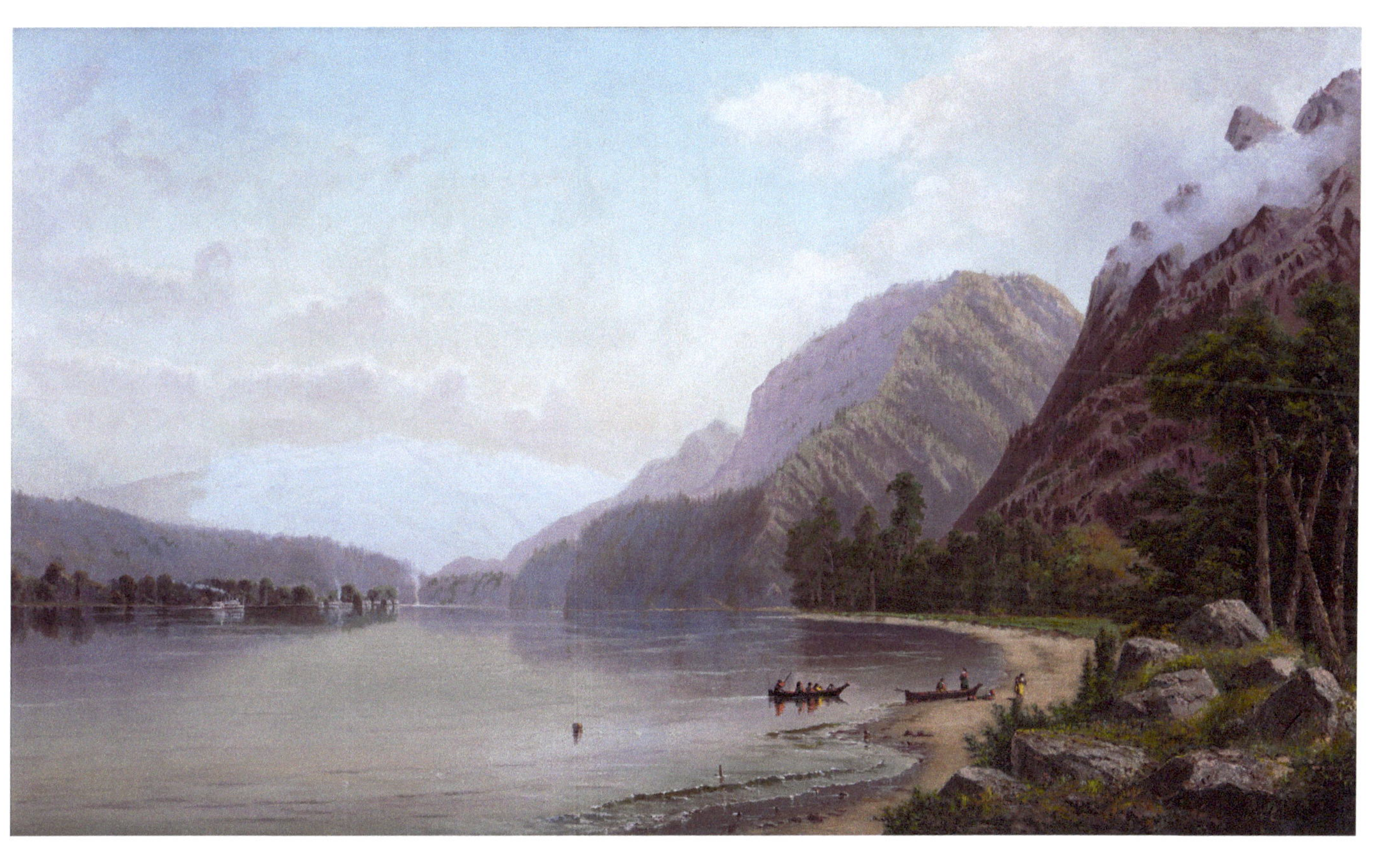

ABOUT THE POET

Michael Czarnecki is a poet, oral memoirist and small press publisher. He founded FootHills Publishing in 1986 and since then FootHills has released over 400 chapbooks and books of poetry. In 1994, Michael gave up other work to devote his time and life to poetry. Since then he has made his living solely through the creative word. In the last 20 years he has given hundreds of featured readings throughout the country.

His *Poems Across America Tour* in 2013, a 14 week journey, featured a reading in each of the 48 contiguous states. Michael has published 15 books, including "Never Stop Asking for Poems" and a haibun account, "Twenty Days on Route 20," of his journey across America on US 20, from Boston to Newport, OR, the longest road in America. When not out on the poetic road, Michael lives with his

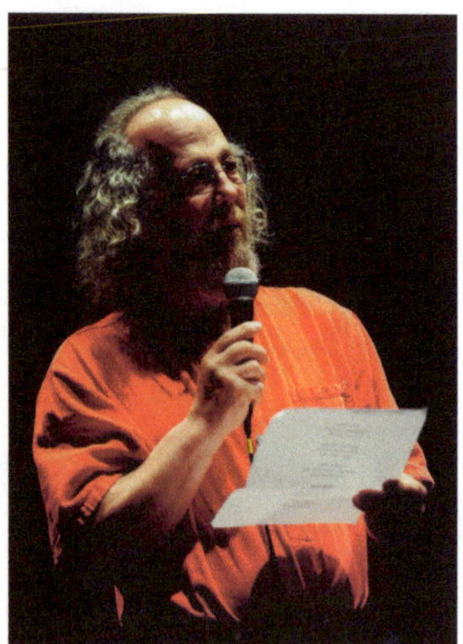

Photograph by Tyler Moore

family on their 50-acre homestead in the northwest portion of the Susquehanna Watershed in New York.

THE ROCKWELL MUSEUM

WHO WE ARE

Located in Corning, New York, The Rockwell Museum is recognized as one of the top museums in the nation through its accreditation by the American Alliance of Museums. Through compelling exhibitions and imaginative programs we seek to provoke curiosity, ignite imagination, challenge perspectives and foster conversation about art and the American experience.

The Rockwell Museum is a proud affiliate of the Smithsonian Institution and a main conduit to Smithsonian collections in Upstate New York. As part of this long-term partnership, The Rockwell and Smithsonian collaborate on a wide variety of projects, including museum exhibitions, public programs and educational opportunities.

Our permanent galleries represent a visual narrative of the American experience. Each space strives to present engaging themes of a collective nature alongside more intimate themes of personal identity. Paintings, drawings, sculpture, photography and objects of material culture have been positioned within an art historical context in order to provide greater cultural interpretation.

HISTORY

Robert 'Bob' Rockwell, Jr. was a consummate collector whose passion for art depicting the American West sprang from his upbringing on a ranch in Colorado. After moving to Corning in 1933 to run his family's department store, Bob and his wife Hertha began collecting paintings that reflected the Western vistas, people and cultures he loved. Unlike many collectors who acquire art for their own enjoyment in private homes, the Rockwells' collection was always intended to be shared with the public as it graced their downtown department store.

With several prominent Western museums vying to be the recipient of the Rockwell collection, Corning city leaders crafted a plan to create a permanent cultural resource for their community. The Houghton family, through their company Corning Glass Works (now Corning Incorporated) pledged to support a museum if the City of Corning would provide a place for it and the Rockwell's would donate their art collection. Corning's historic City Hall, vacant after the flood caused by Hurricane Agnes in 1972, was chosen as the ultimate location, but as it required major renovation and updates, the newly created Rockwell-Corning Museum opened in 1976 in the

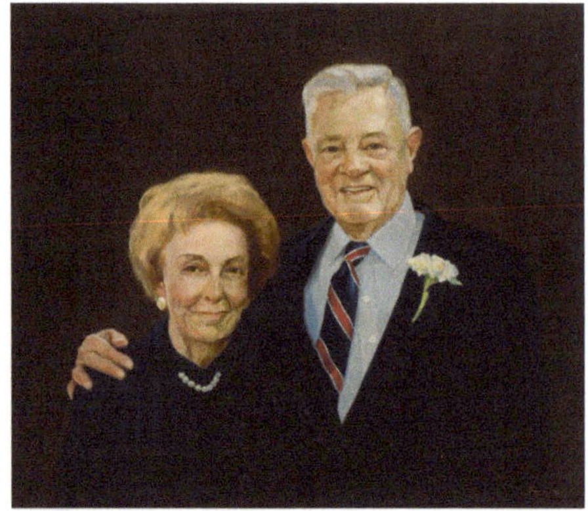

Thomas S. Buechner, Portrait of Robert F. Rockwell, Jr. and Hertha Rockwell, 2004, oil on canvas, 28 1/4 × 32 1/8 in. Gift of Thomas S. Buechner. 2004.2.

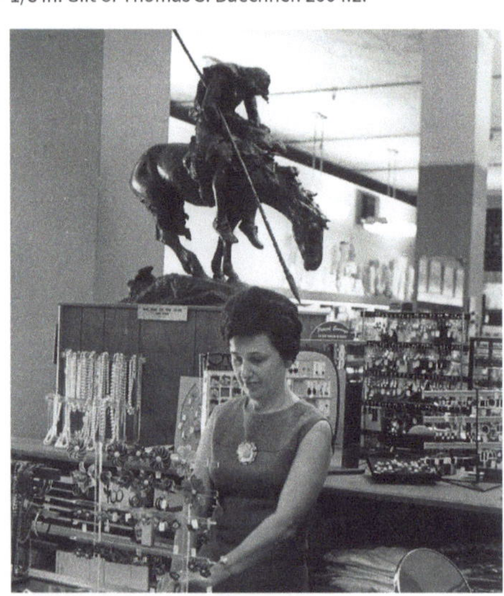

The Rockwells' collection was first on view in their downtown department store.

Baron Steuben Hotel in downtown Corning, NY, as a Bicentennial gift to the community.

In 1982, the Museum consolidated its name to The Rockwell Museum and moved into its permanent home at Old City Hall, a major project of adaptive reuse for a community where historic preservation is a cornerstone of its identity. The many adjacent buildings along Market Street were also renovated and adapted in the 1970s as one of the earliest Main Street revitalization projects in the country, turning factories and bars into retail, residential and restaurant spaces that give Corning its charming character.

Old City Hall had long served Corning as a community center and housed not only the fire department, dentist office, city jail and administrative offices but of course was the location for celebrations, weddings and public dances. From the original makeup of floors and space, the Museum created galleries, education spaces and offices. In 2018, Old City Hall celebrated its 125th birthday with exhibitions both in the Museum and community highlighting its history and former life.

As many museums continue to adjust their purpose to fit the expectation of the 21st century visitor, The Rockwell builds on its roots as a community center and utilizes its resources to connect underserved communities in the region to the collection through exceptional programs and art experiences. Arts in education is a major avenue of programming ensuring the museum experience is both dynamic and reflective of contemporary expectation.

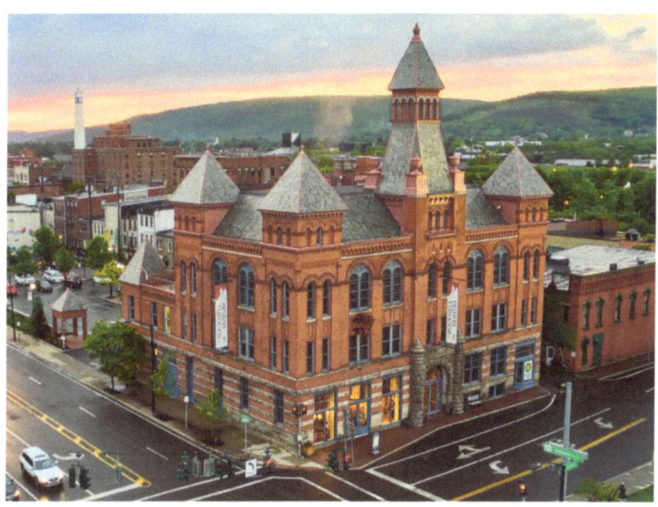

Aerial view of The Rockwell Museum, housed in Corning's historic City Hall. Photograph by Brian Maloney.